RATE THE CUTENESS!

THE CUTEST

ANIMAL BABIES

MORTIMER

I AM A BEAR

Brown bears eat **just about anything!**
They most often eat nuts, berries, leaves, and roots,
but won't say no if a salmon ≋**leaps** into their <u>**JAWS!**</u>

CUTENESS ALERT!

Cute and cuddly bear cubs stay with their mom until they are around two and a half years old. She usually has up to four cubs at a time—what a furry handful!

WE ARE BEAR CUBS!

Mom teaches her babies how to find food and where to sleep.

Seals are covered with a **thick layer of fat** called **BLUBBER**, which keeps them warm in even the coldest seas. Some seals can **dive** up to half a mile deep.

CUTENESS ALERT!

Baby seals can make a special cry for their moms, and their moms can recognize their own pups' calls even after five years apart.

Seal pups are such good swimmers, they can even doze off in the water! It's a good thing they can hold their breath for up to two hours!

I AM A SEAL PUP!

I AM A TIGER

Tigers are the world's **largest big cats**—they're even **BIGGER** than lions! They're also one of the only big cats that like being in ≋ **water** ≋ and they're excellent swimmers.

CUTENESS ALERT!
Tiger cubs don't open their eyes for six to twelve days after they're born.

RATE THE CUTENESS!

WE ARE TIGER CUBS!

By the time tiger cubs are four months old, they're as big as a medium-sized dog! When they're eight months old, their mom teaches them to hunt.

Elephants are the world's **largest** animals on land. That means their babies are **SUPERSIZE cute**! Everyone in the herd helps take care of the babies.

RATE THE CUTENESS!

CUTENESS ALERT!
Baby elephants hold onto their mommy's tail with their trunk.

Baby elephants will suck their trunk, just like human babies suck their thumb!

Pandas spend up to **16 hours a day eating BAMBOO**! They have a special wristbone that they use like a thumb, to help hold the stalks.

RATE THE CUTENESS!

CUTENESS ALERT!
Newborn pandas are tiny. They're 900 times smaller than their mother!

Panda moms never let go of their babies for the first month, keeping them snuggled up close.

I'M A PANDA CUB!

I AM A RABBIT

Rabbits have ⟲**360 degree vision**, to spot <u>**DANGER**</u> from every angle. They can produce up to **seven** babies in one litter, and they can have a litter *every month* in the breeding season!

CUTENESS ALERT!
Rabbits' teeth never stop growing! Gnawing on their food keeps their teeth the right length.

A mother rabbit is called a doe, and a baby rabbit is called a kit.

Marine turtles can **swim up to 20 miles a day**. Turtle babies are tiny, but when they grow up, they weigh up to **HALF A TON**!

Turtles always return to the same beach they hatched on, to lay their own eggs.

RATE THE CUTENESS!

CUTENESS ALERT!
When their eggs hatch, the tiny new hatchlings have to make their way back into the sea all by themselves.

I'M A HATCHLING!

17

I AM A **DEER**

Deer can be found all around the world (except Antarctica—brr!) There are **over 60 species** of deer, and they are the only creatures in the world to have **ANTLERS**.

CUTENESS ALERT!
Most fawns have white spots on their back for camouflage.
As they grow older, the spots disappear.

WE ARE FAWNS!

Fawns learn to walk half an hour after they're born!

There are over **330 breeds of dog**. A dog's sense of smell is at least 40 times as sensitive as a human's—over 1000 times for some species!

CUTENESS ALERT!
Just like humans, puppies have baby teeth which they grow out of!

The largest litter ever recorded was 24 puppies. That's a lot of cuddles!

I AM A PUPPY!

Sheep can recognize up to **50 individual human (and sheep) faces**! Perhaps it's because they're **super social** animals who form **strong FRIENDSHIPS** with each other.

CUTENESS ALERT!
Lambs love racing, leaping and even play-fighting with each other!

RATE THE CUTENESS!

I AM A LAMB!

One pound of sheep's wool can make ten miles of yarn.

I AM A PENGUIN

You'll only find penguins in the **Southern Hemisphere**. Although they're *happiest* in the water, they can travel quickly on ice by lying on their bellies and **sliding**!

CUTENESS ALERT!

In the water, a group of penguins is called a raft. But on land, they're called a waddle!

WE ARE PENGUIN CHICKS!

Emperor penguins don't build nests. They carry their eggs on their feet to keep them warm.

I AM A FOX

You'll find foxes **all around the world**. They *love* deep forests, but they can also be found in some towns and cities, where humans leave tasty scraps for them to steal.

CUTENESS ALERT!
Baby foxes live in a den with their parents until they're seven months old, but they love to go out at dawn or dusk and enjoy rough-and-tumble play.

I'M A FOX CUB!

Baby foxes are called cubs, but they're also known as kits or kittens!

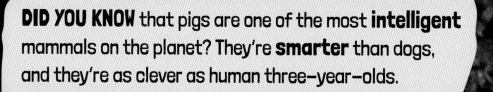

DID YOU KNOW that pigs are one of the most **intelligent** mammals on the planet? They're **smarter** than dogs, and they're as clever as human three-year-olds.

I AM A PIG

Mommy pigs make a singing sound to calm their babies.

I'M A PIGLET!

CUTENESS ALERT!

Piglets are very curious and inquisitive, and they love to play with toys. In fact, they never grow out of it! Even adult pigs love playing with toys, using tools, and even learning tricks.

29

Sloths **snooze for about 15 hours every day**. And when they're awake, they move incredibly slowly—only about 40 yards **A DAY**.
They only come down from their trees once a week, to poop!